What Happens When I Have a Skin Condition?

Emiliya King

PowerKiDS press

Published in 2026 by The Rosen Publishing Group, Inc.
2544 Clinton Street, Buffalo, NY 14224

Copyright © 2026 by The Rosen Publishing Group, Inc.

First Edition

All rights reserved. No part of this book may be reproduced in any form without permission in writing from the publisher, except by a reviewer.

Editor: Caitie McAneney
Book Design: Leslie Taylor

Photo Credits: Cover Savicic/Shutterstock.com; p. 5 Zoriana Zaitseva/Shutterstock.com; p. 7 New Africa/Shutterstock.com; p. 9 (albino) Shakirov Albert/Shutterstock.com, (vitiligo inset) alinabuphoto/Shutterstock.com; p. 11 Maryna Kulchytska/Shutterstock.com; p. 13 Aisylu Ahmadieva/Shutterstock.com; p. 15 Trzykropy/Shutterstock.com; p. 17 vk_st/Shutterstock.com; p. 19 Kamil Macniak/Shutterstock.com; p. 21 Chay_Tee/Shutterstock.com.

Cataloging-in-Publication Data
Names: King, Emiliya.
Title: What happens when I have a skin condition? / Emiliya King.
Description: Buffalo, NY : PowerKids Press, 2026. | Series: What happens next? dealing with life changes| Includes glossary and index.
Identifiers: ISBN 9781499452631 (pbk.) | ISBN 9781499452648 (library bound) | ISBN 9781499452655 (ebook)
Subjects: LCSH: Skin–Diseases–Juvenile literature. | Skin–Juvenile literature.
Classification: LCC RL86.K46 2026 | DDC 616.5–dc23

Manufactured in the United States of America

Some of the images in this book illustrate individuals who are models. The depictions do not imply actual situations or events.

CPSIA Compliance Information: Batch #CSPK26. For Further Information contact Rosen Publishing at 1-800-237-9932.

CONTENTS

What Are Skin Conditions? 4
That's Itchy! 6
Seeing Spots 8
Marks on the Skin 10
Skin Infections 12
Getting Comfortable 14
Medicines Can Help 16
Your Support Team 18
Feeling Confident 20
Glossary 22
For More Information 23
Index 24

What Are Skin Conditions?

Your skin has an important job. It holds everything in your body together. It allows a sense of touch, keeps body parts safe, and keeps you at a good temperature. But if you have a skin condition, your skin might make you uncomfortable, in both body and mind.

Some skin conditions are temporary, such as rashes or **infections**. Others are lifelong, such as those that affect skin **pigment**. This book will give you the tools to understand and deal with your skin condition.

A dermatologist is a skin doctor. They will look at your skin closely to help treat you.

Your Point of View

Skin is the largest organ in the human body. That's why having a widespread rash or itch on your skin can be very uncomfortable!

That's Itchy!

Some skin conditions cause itching. Eczema is a common skin condition that involves dry, itchy skin. It's also called atopic dermatitis. You may see bumpy, scaly, red skin. It may get worse at night. Hives also include red, itchy bumps. Itchy rashes may be **triggered** by **allergies**, heat, or certain things that touch the skin.

Dealing with itchy skin can be hard! Putting on special creams and lotions can help heal your skin. Other creams may stop the itching for a while.

Your Point of View

Some people call eczema "the itch that rashes." The more you scratch, the worse it gets.

Try not to scratch your skin. You can cover it with clothing or bandages, or try to put your attention on something else.

Seeing Spots

Pigment is another word for the color of your skin. Skin gets its pigment from melanin. The more melanin a person has, the darker their skin will look. Most people have skin pigment that is the same over the whole body.

However, some people lose pigment in parts of their skin, causing white patches and spots. This is a skin condition called vitiligo. No one knows what causes vitiligo for sure, but **stress** may make it worse.

Having vitiligo or albinism may make you look different from others. But you can celebrate your differences and the pigment of your skin!

Your Point of View

Albinism is a condition in which a person lacks melanin. They have very light skin, hair, and eyes, and need to be very careful in the sun.

9

Marks on the Skin

Many people have marks on the skin that make them **unique**, such as freckles, moles, and scars. Some people are born with darker spots and patches of skin, often called birthmarks.

Usually, marks on the skin are nothing to worry about, and a dermatologist can check them out if anything seems "off." New or growing moles should be checked to make sure they're not skin **cancer**. Some people may feel **self-conscious** about marks on their skin. Over time, you can learn to accept the things that make you unique.

Some birthmarks are brown, tan, purple, or pink.
Some get smaller or go away over time, while others stay.

Your Point of View

Some birthmarks are flat, while others are raised.
They can be anywhere on the body.

Skin Infections

Infections of the skin can be caused by viruses, bacteria, and **fungi**. If you have hard bumps on your skin, they may be warts, which are caused by a virus. If you have a cut or rash that starts to get red, painful, and swollen, it may be a bacterial infection. Ring-shaped rashes are often ringworm, which is a fungal infection.

A doctor will tell you what kind of infection you have. Then, they can give you a medicine to take by mouth or a cream to put on your skin.

> Bacterial infections happen when germs make their way into the skin. That's why it's important to keep cuts and burns covered up and clean.

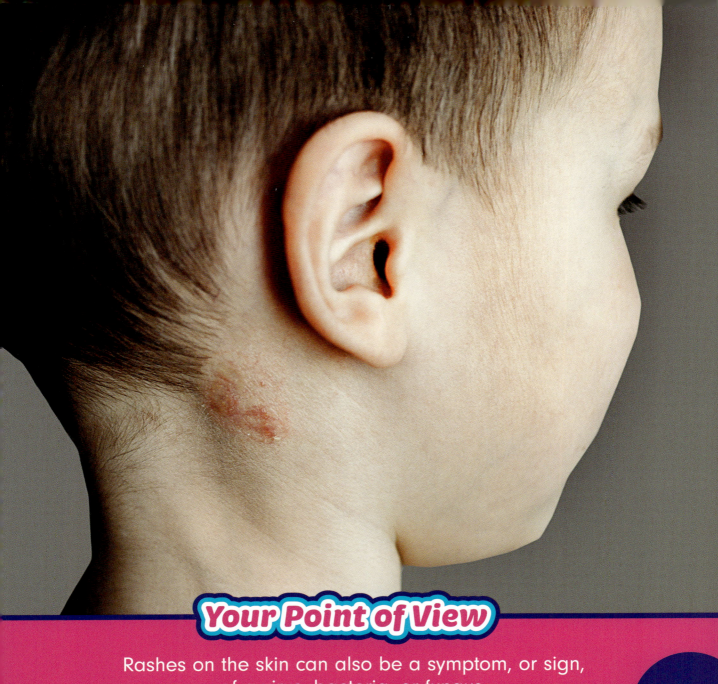

Your Point of View

Rashes on the skin can also be a symptom, or sign, of a virus, bacteria, or fungus.

13

Getting Comfortable

If you get rashes and skin discomfort, you can make some changes in your life to be more comfortable. Light and airy clothes are best for the skin. Plain, loose cotton clothing allows the skin to "breathe."

Try to stay away from irritants, or things that trigger your skin condition. People who are allergic to pets, pollen, and certain foods can keep away from them. You can also clean sheets and clothing with **detergents** that don't smell or have harmful chemicals.

Using simple, gentle soaps and detergents can keep your skin from itching or turning red.

Your Point of View

Clothes made of wool and synthetic (man-made) cloth sometimes cause skin to heat up and itch.

Medicines Can Help

A dermatologist can usually give you the right medicine to help your skin clear up or lessen any itching or redness. Antibiotics may be used to treat skin infections, while antifungals treat skin conditions caused by fungi. Treating the issue in your body that caused the condition should help your skin clear up.

Some medicines are topical, or put directly on the skin. These creams help the skin heal. They also bring comfort when skin is itchy and swollen. Other medicines are taken by mouth.

Your Point of View

If you have a virus, your skin may clear on its own after you've gotten better.

Always ask your parents before using a cream, even if it's a lotion that you find at home. You need the right one for your skin.

Your Support Team

You are not alone if you have a skin condition! There are many other kids who deal with these issues, whether they are short-lived flare-ups or lifelong pigment differences. You can connect with other kids with this issue and read more about it so you don't feel so alone.

You also have your support team. Your doctors can help you by checking your skin and giving you medicine. Your parents can help you stay comfortable with the right clothes, soaps, and detergents.

Your Point of View

You may feel worried to open up about your skin condition, but talking with friends and family can help.

If you have discomfort, pain, or worries about your skin, your caregivers and doctors can help you.

Feeling Confident

Skin conditions can be hard to deal with because of **physical** discomfort. However, sometimes how you feel about your looks can be the hardest part.

Remember that everyone looks different—and that's okay! There's not one "perfect" picture of beauty. Also, your looks—including your skin pigment, marks, or rashes—are the least interesting thing about you. You are still *you* even if you have a skin condition. Find friends who accept you for who you are. Feel confident in your own skin!

Many people see their vitiligo as a cool and unique **trait**!

Your Point of View

Ask yourself: who am I, apart from my skin condition? Maybe you're a great runner, a good friend, or a singer. Your skin condition can't take that from you.

Glossary

allergy: A bad bodily reaction to certain foods, animals, or surroundings.

cancer: A disease caused by the uncontrolled growth of cells in the body.

detergent: Something that can clean something else, especially cloth.

fungus: A living thing that's like a plant but that doesn't have leaves, flowers, or green color or make its own food. The plural form is fungi.

infection: A sickness caused by germs entering the body.

physical: Having to do with the body.

pigment: A natural coloring matter in living things.

self-conscious: Feeling uncomfortably nervous or embarrassed when in the presence of or when being observed by other people.

stress: Something that causes strong feelings of worry.

trait: A quality that makes one person or thing different from another.

trigger: Something that sets off another thing.

unique: Special or one of a kind.

For More Information

Books

Rivera, Lid-ya C. *I Absolutely, Positively Love My Spots*. New York, NY: HarperCollins Publishers, 2023.

Wallace, Amy. *What Happens When I Have a Serious Allergy?* Buffalo, NY: PowerKids Press, 2025.

Websites

Eczema
kidshealth.org/en/kids/eczema.html
Learn more about eczema with KidsHealth.

Vitiligo
kids.kiddle.co/Vitiligo
This resource may answer other questions you have about vitiligo.

Publisher's note to educators and parents: Our editors have carefully reviewed these websites to ensure that they are suitable for students. Many websites change frequently, however, and we cannot guarantee that a site's future contents will continue to meet our high standards of quality and educational value. Be advised that students should be closely supervised whenever they access the internet.

Index

A
albinism, 8, 9
allergies, 6, 14

B
birthmarks, 10, 11

C
clothing, 7, 14, 15, 18

D
dermatologist, 5, 10, 16
detergents, 14, 15, 18

E
eczema, 6

I
infection, 4, 12, 16
irritants, 14

M
medicine, 12, 16, 18
moles, 10

P
pigment, 4, 8, 18, 20

R
rash, 4, 5, 6, 13, 14, 20

S
scars, 10
skin cancer, 10
stress, 8
support team, 18

V
vitiligo, 8, 21